I0828197

THIS BOOK BELONGS TO:

WELCOME TO MASSACHUSETTS

Dedicated to all the explorers.

ISBN 978-1-958985-99-1

www.joeysavestheday.com

Mimi Books™ Publishing

A Mimi Book

Massachusetts got its name from the Massachusett people, a Native American nation whose name means "near the great hill." Early English settlers adopted the name when they arrived in the 1600s. Over time, "Massachusetts" became the official name of the state we know today, known for its history, coastline, and colorful seasons.

Massachusetts has a long history that begins with Native American nations who lived along its coast and forests for thousands of years. English settlers arrived in the early 1600s and founded some of the first towns in America. The state later became an important center of the American Revolution, with famous events like the Boston Tea Party. Today, Massachusetts stands proudly as one of the original 13 states, celebrated for its historic cities, stunning coastline, and vibrant cultural heritage.

Massachusetts was the sixth state to join the Union. It officially joined on February 6, 1788.

6th

Massachusetts is located in the northeastern United States. It is bordered by New York, Vermont, New Hampshire, Connecticut, and Rhode Island. It also touches the Atlantic Ocean along its eastern coast.

Boston is the capital of Massachusetts. It officially became the capital in 1630.

Boston, Massachusetts, has an estimated population of about 654,000 people.
Massachusetts

Massachusetts is the forty-fourth largest state in the United States by area.

Salem, Massachusetts

There are approximately 7,100,000 people residing in the state of Massachusetts.

Rockport, Massachusetts

John Adams was born in Braintree, Massachusetts in 1735 and became one of America's most important Founding Fathers. He helped lead the country during the American Revolution and later became the 2nd President of the United States. Adams believed strongly in fairness, education, and independence. He worked hard to help the colonies become a free nation, and his ideas helped shape the early government of the United States.

Massachusetts is known for its delicious cranberries, especially the ones grown in the state's famous bogs. These bright red berries are tart, flavorful, and used to make juices, sauces, and sweet treats. Families across Massachusetts enjoy cranberries during holidays and festivals, and they've become one of the state's most traditional and beloved foods.

MASSACHUSETTS

There are 14 counties in Massachusetts.

Here is a list of those counties:

Barnstable	Essex	Middlesex	Suffolk
Berkshire	Franklin	Nantucket	Worcester
Bristol	Hampden	Norfolk	
Dukes	Hampshire	Plymouth	

Lulu Cascade is a charming little waterfall hidden in the woods of Pittsfield, Massachusetts. The water flows gently over rocky steps and into a quiet forest stream, creating a peaceful spot for families to explore. The cascade sits near the historic site of the old Lulu amusement park, which once brought visitors to the area in the early 1900s.

One of the most famous moments in Massachusetts history is the Boston Tea Party, which took place in 1773. Colonists in Boston were upset about unfair taxes on tea, so they boarded ships in the harbor and tipped the tea into the water as a bold protest. This event became an important spark that helped lead to the American Revolution. Today, the Boston Harbor is still known for this historic act of courage and the role it played in shaping the United States.

The Leonard P. Zakim Bunker Hill Memorial Bridge stands in the heart of Boston, carrying traffic along Interstate 93. The bridge crosses the Charles River with its tall, cable-stayed towers that look a bit like sails. Opened in 2003, it helps thousands of travelers, commuters, and families move smoothly through the busy city each day.

The Massachusetts state bird is the Black-capped Chickadee. It was chosen as the state bird in 1941.

The official state flower of Massachusetts is the Mayflower. It was chosen as the state flower in 1918.

Massachusetts' nickname is the Bay State.

THE

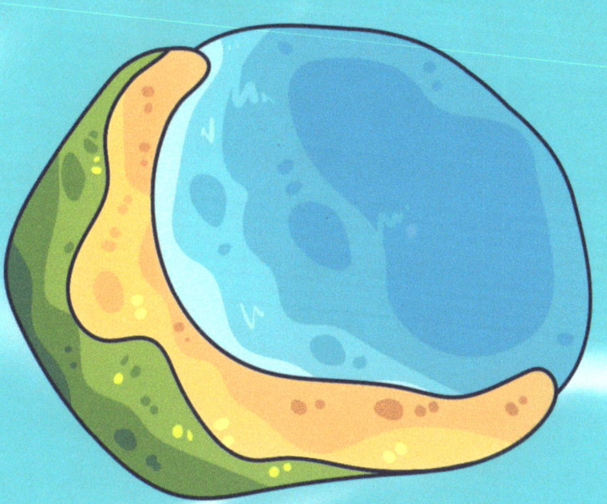

ST8

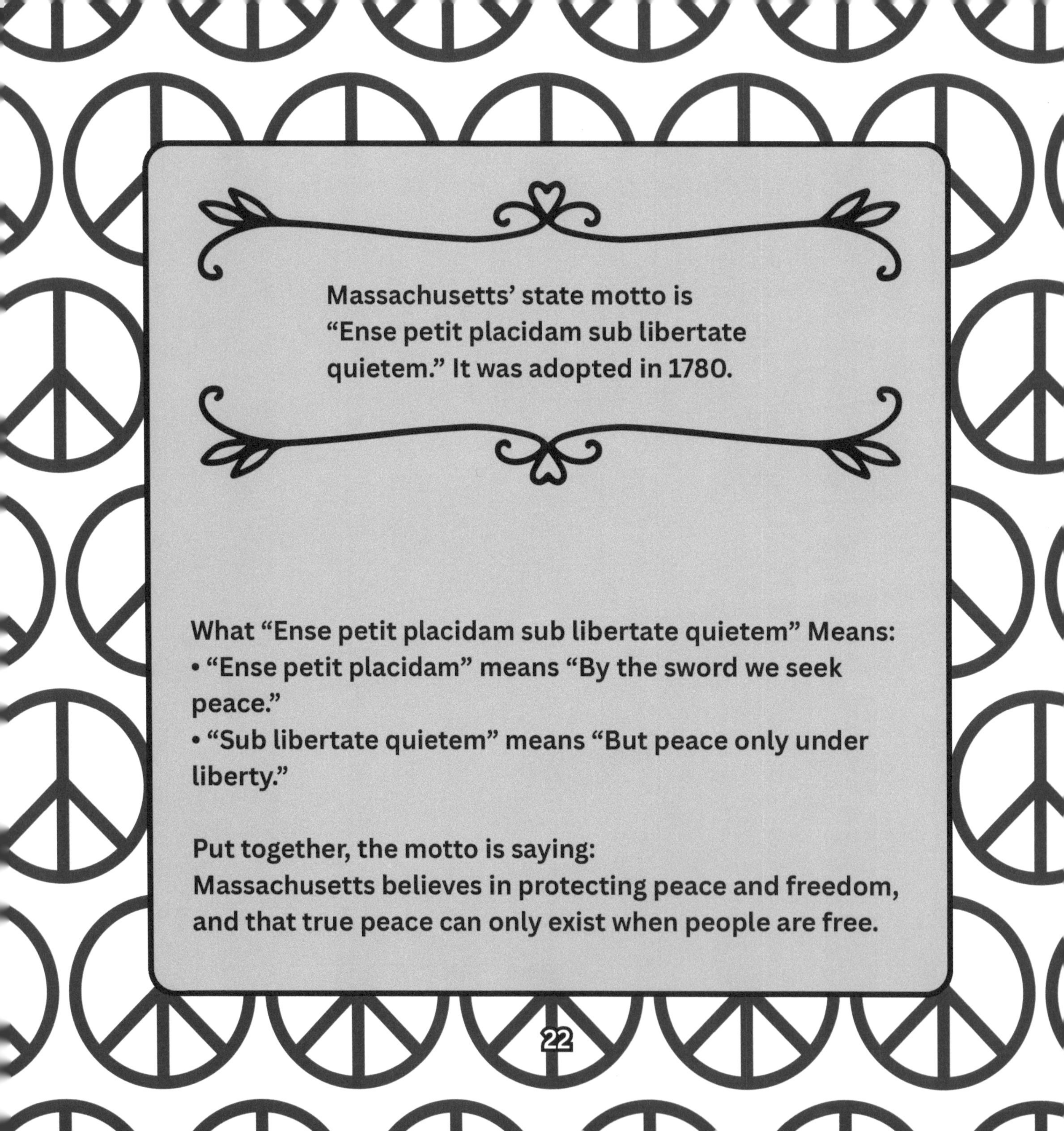

Massachusetts' state motto is "Ense petit placidam sub libertate quietem." It was adopted in 1780.

What "Ense petit placidam sub libertate quietem" Means:

- "Ense petit placidam" means "By the sword we seek peace."
- "Sub libertate quietem" means "But peace only under liberty."

Put together, the motto is saying:
Massachusetts believes in protecting peace and freedom, and that true peace can only exist when people are free.

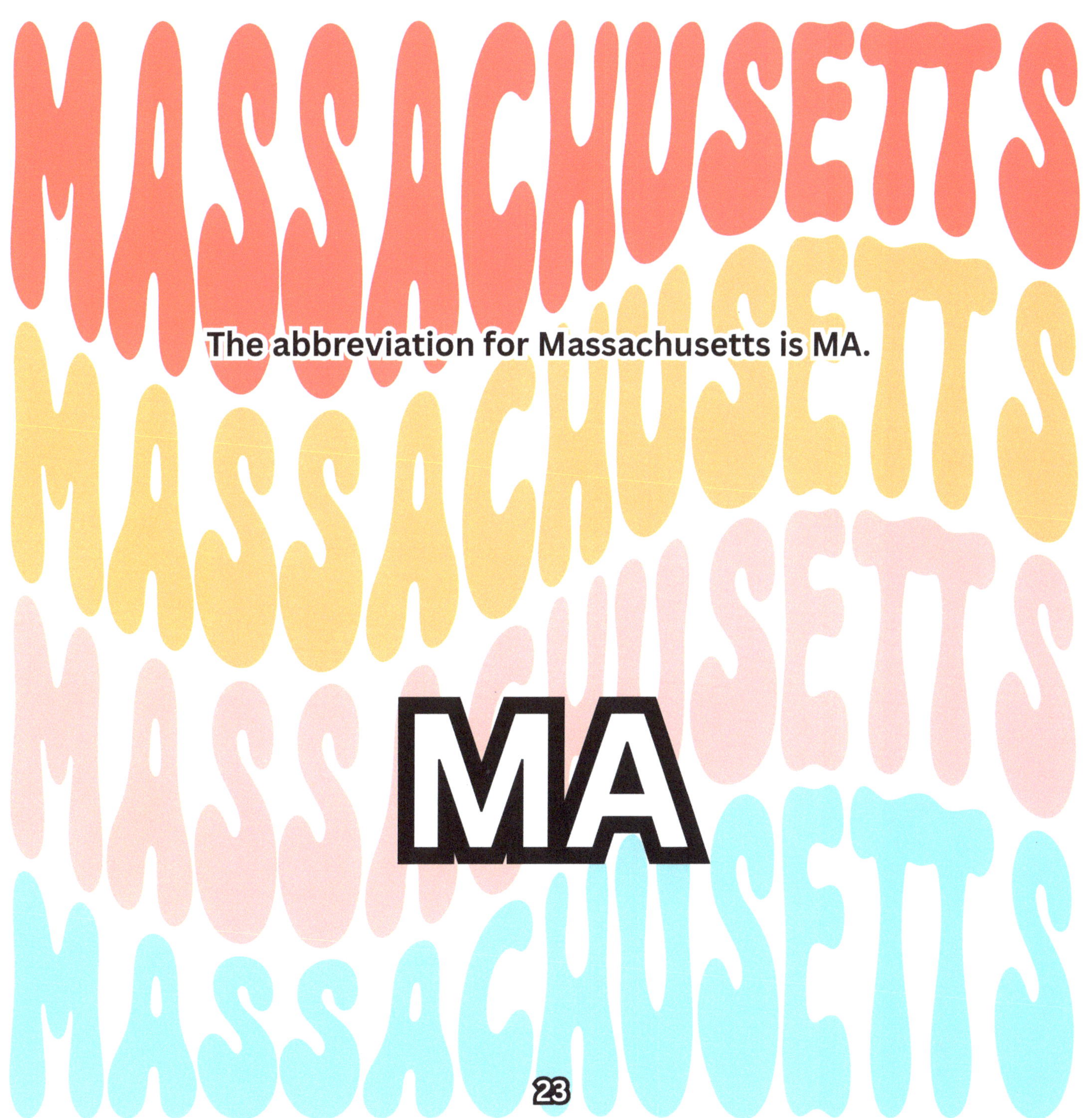

The abbreviation for Massachusetts is MA.

MA

Massachusetts' state flag was officially adopted in 1915.

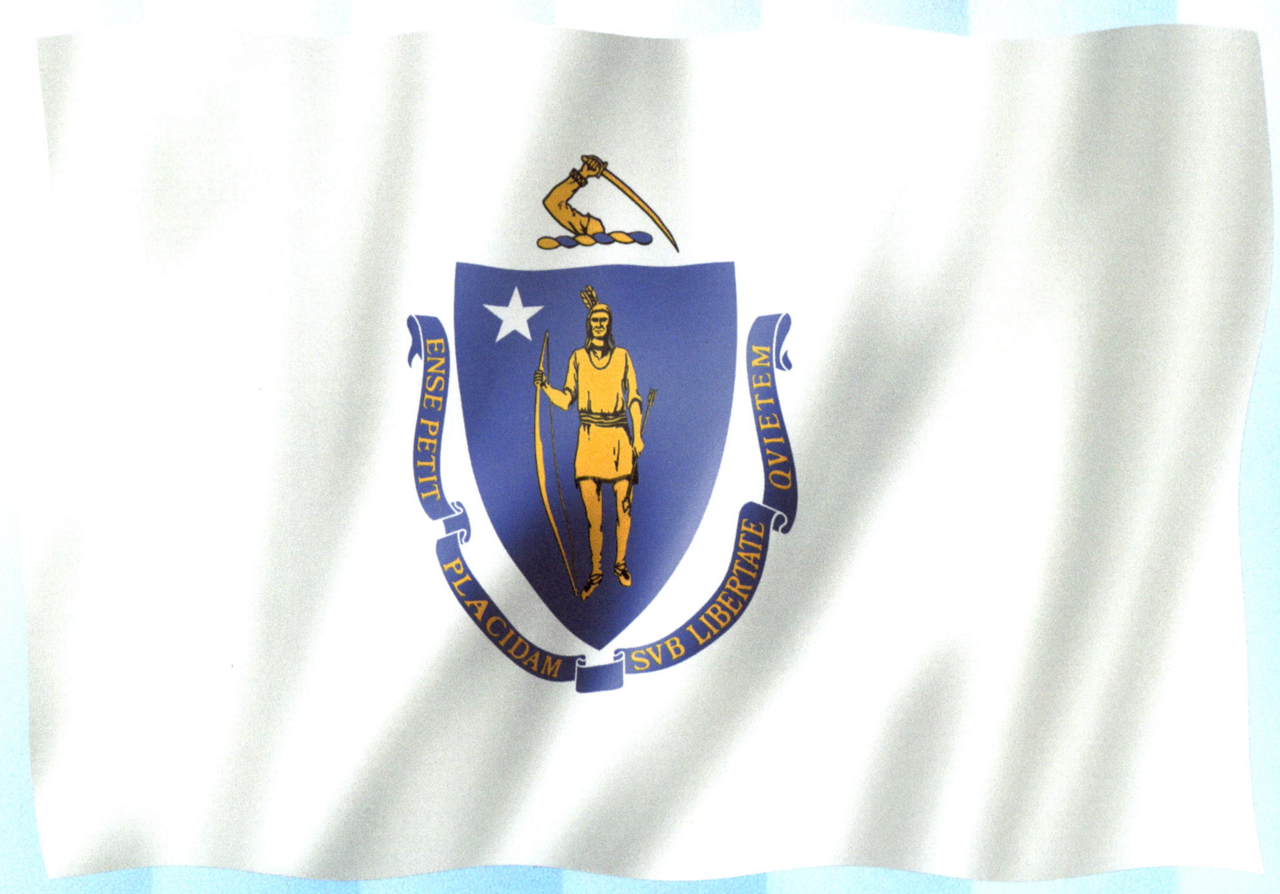

Some crops grown in Massachusetts are cranberries, apples, corn, and potatoes.

Some animals that live in Massachusetts are white-tailed deer, black bears, red foxes, eastern cottontails, and harbor seals.

Massachusetts experiences a wide range of temperatures throughout the year. The hottest temperature ever recorded in the state was 107 degrees Fahrenheit, measured in New Bedford on August 2, 1975. In contrast, the coldest temperature documented was −40 degrees Fahrenheit, recorded in Chester on January 22, 1984.

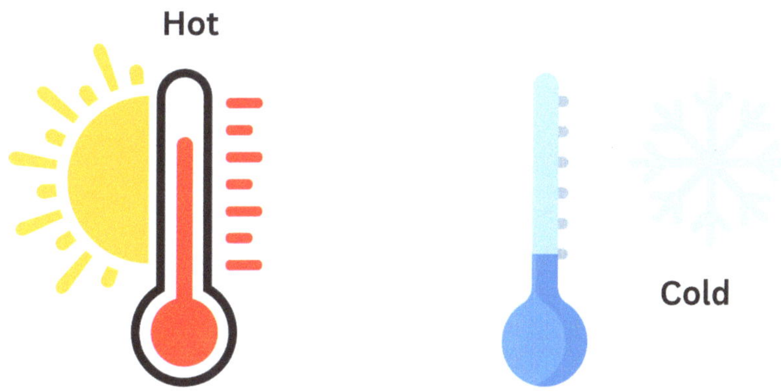

The Franklin Park Zoo in Boston is a wonderful place to explore, with animals from all around the world. Kids can see lions, tigers, giraffes, red pandas, and playful primates, along with colorful birds and reptiles.

Elias Howe was an inventor from Massachusetts who created one of the first successful sewing machines. His ideas helped people sew clothing faster and easier. People remember him for his creativity, hard work, and inventions that changed how things were made.

The largest airport in Massachusetts is Logan International Airport, located in Boston. It sits at 1 Harborside Drive and serves as the main travel hub for people flying in and out of Massachusetts. This airport connects travelers to cities all across the country and to destinations around the world, making it one of the busiest and most important airports in New England.

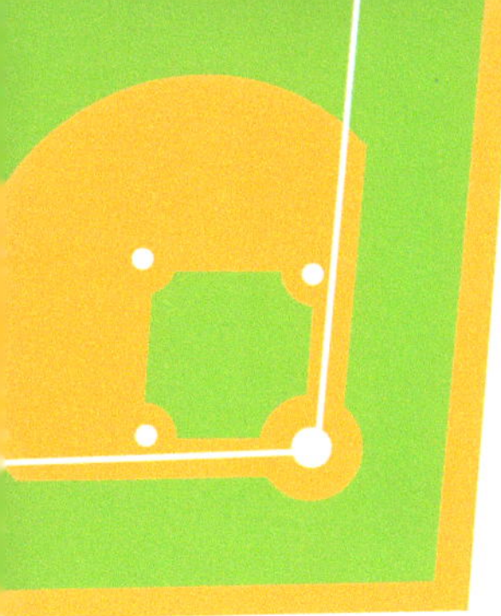

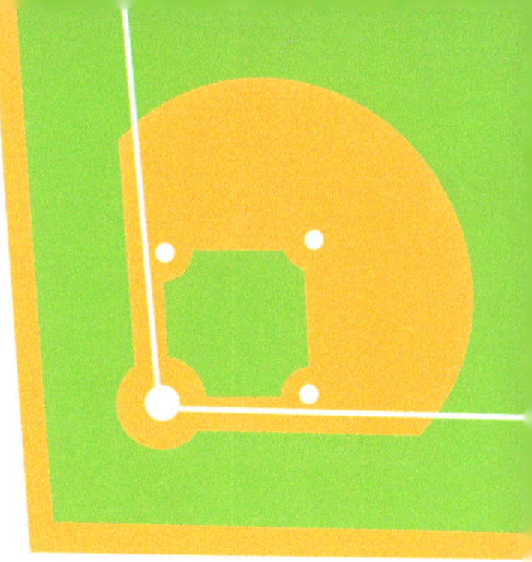

The Boston Red Sox are a Major League Baseball team based in Boston, one of Massachusetts' most famous and historic cities. They play their home games at Fenway Park, a bright and energetic ballpark known for its classic charm, enthusiastic fans, and the iconic Green Monster towering over left field. The Red Sox are one of the oldest teams in baseball, and many talented players have worn their uniform as they built their skills and made baseball history.

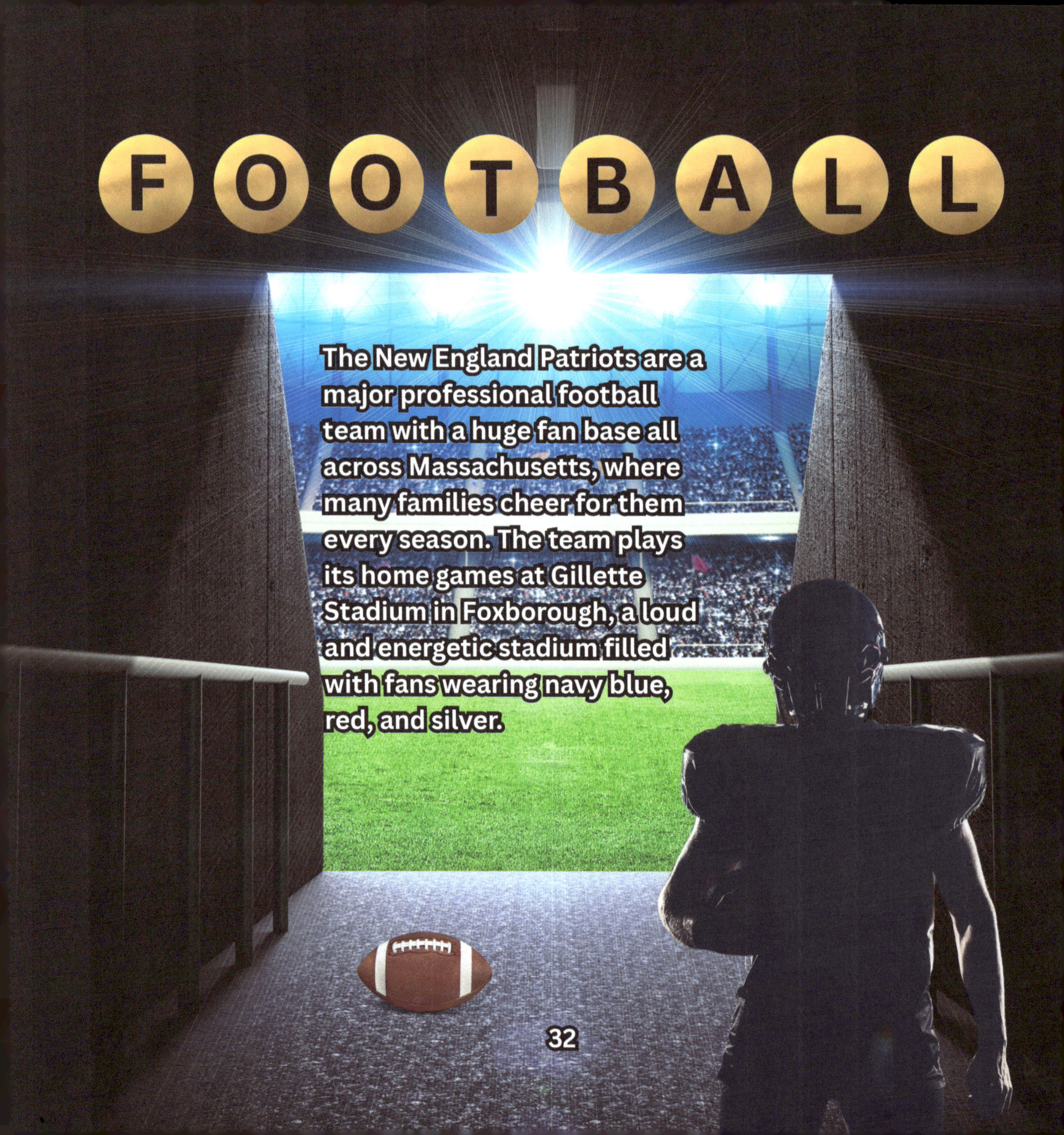

FOOTBALL

The New England Patriots are a major professional football team with a huge fan base all across Massachusetts, where many families cheer for them every season. The team plays its home games at Gillette Stadium in Foxborough, a loud and energetic stadium filled with fans wearing navy blue, red, and silver.

The American elm is Massachusetts' state tree. It's known for its tall, graceful shape and its arching branches that create a beautiful canopy of leaves in the summer. The American elm was officially adopted as the state tree in 1941.

The Atlantic cod is Massachusetts' state fish. It's a sleek, silver-brown fish known for its gentle shape and the little barbel, or "whisker," under its chin. The Atlantic cod was officially adopted as the state fish in 1974, and it has long been an important symbol of Massachusetts' history and coastal fishing traditions.

Can you name these?

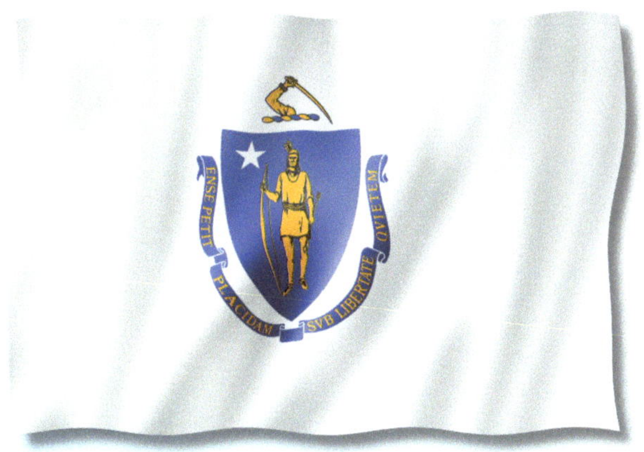

I hope you enjoyed
learning about
Massachusetts.

To explore fun facts about the other 49 states, visit my website at www.joeysavestheday.com. You'll also find a wide variety of homeschool resources to support joyful learning at home. If you enjoyed this book, I would be grateful if you left a review. Your feedback truly helps.
Thank you for your support!

Check out these other interesting books in the 50 States Fact Books Series!

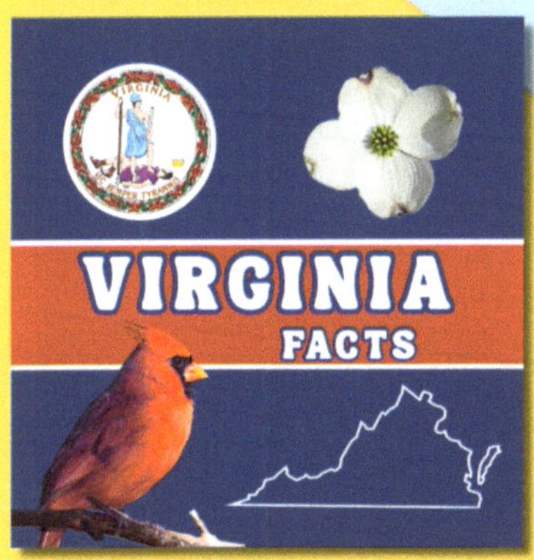

www.mimibooks.com

www.ingramcontent.com/pod-product-compliance
Lightning Source LLC
LaVergne TN
LVHW070200110826
845147LV00002B/456

* 9 7 8 1 9 5 8 9 8 5 9 9 1 *